Yeah, I Said It, I Don't Give a D.A.M.N.

Addressing:
Disparities
Allegiances
Mindsets
N-words

Chanae Jackson
The Accidental Activist ™

Yeah, I Said It, I Don't Give a D.A.M.N.
Copyright © 2021 by Chanae Jackson

ISBN (978-1-73753-106-7)

MTE Publishing
mtepublishing.com

Dedication

I dedicate this literary work/call to action to my children, my daddy and "my people" (you know who you are). To my cousin, Erika, thank you for every time you stayed in my ear about the things you knew I were purposed FOR but didn't want to hear!

To every person that has pushed me, encouraged me, inspired me, heard me, and listened to me, I am forever grateful. My words will never have the capacity to completely express my appreciation. This book, "Yeah, I Said It, I Don't Give a D.A.M.N." is for you!

Foreword

By Angela "Angie" Nixon,
Florida House of Representatives

I have been a community organizer and intentional activist for more than a decade. Consequently, my career allows me to work with underrepresented and underserved communities, purposely. I realize establishing relationships is essential to building capacity with the people we serve. However, community activism requires work beyond lip service. We must go into the suburbs and the *'hoods* to connect with other entrepreneurs, educational leaders, and political leaders. People must be met where they are… so we can connect, educate, and ensure understanding that renders beneficial outcomes within activism.

I am openly supporting "Yeah, I Said It, I Don't Give a D.A.M.N.," because I see myself in Ms. Jackson and the work/change she is committed to. I understand that power can and will shift, especially when Black and brown people strategically collaborate and hold those in power accountable. Therefore, we must understand that

iv

change requires more than performative acts. It demands that those in power STOP just looking the part and be the part.

This book will help readers understand how to become and be an INTENTIONAL activist. Hopefully, readers will move from complacency, to collaboration, and ultimately communal and worldwide change. Our communities no longer need to simply survive, but we must thrive. We deserve every opportunity to FLOURISH, and this starts with everyone simply giving a damn!

Table of Contents

Introduction

Accidentally Accepted, Intentionally Chosen

I stumbled into this whole activist thing [turned calling]. By nature, I like to remain behind the scenes; it's where I'm most comfortable. However, I was there [in the midst of social activism] to learn. I realized the people in power [the experts] had a lot to learn from those who are being impacted [those suppressed]. I was frustrated at the disconnect and it was triggering. People who make decisions often have superficial conversations with those being impacted. These conversations transpire for the sake of saying they "happened." I realized we have been bred to shut up and be quiet and allow others to speak for us. But they *don't* know us, and more importantly they don't seek to understand us. Even when we consider the disciplinary actions taken towards Black children. Brown students are suspended more often for asking questions and it's considered insubordination.

We love our children obsessively because we know what society will do to them [eat them alive and shoot them dead]. And just because we don't "show up," this doesn't mean we don't care. However, it sheds light on the fact that when we do show up... we are dismissed, ignored, and often seen as the problem instead of those in need of help! We're simply trying to survive.

I was at a "Black on Black" task force meeting; they were talking about the youth and discussing "their" programs and initiatives. However, none of the youth were present and neither were the parents. Everyone talked about "their" programs. I thought to myself...*all of these programs are reactive but not proactive.* By the time these kids are involved they've already been labeled problematic, which causes them to be perceived as lost causes.

At the onset of my activism, as a single mom, I realized what I was being called to was much bigger than me and my sons; and although I am not a superhero, I knew if I kept speaking, my voice would be [and IS] just as powerful!

I searched for preventative programs long before this meeting. My sons were sheltered, and I was proactively trying to save them. So, when I saw signs of deviation from what I had instilled in my sons, I rushed to find help because I wasn't going to lose them– to the system, to the streets, to themselves, or anything else. Nevertheless, the programs I found only offered support to kids who were already in trouble. Trouble was a prerequisite for acceptance and positive behavior was the prerequisite for dismissal. I was told by program facilitators to "stay the course". I had to fight tooth and nail to protect my sons. Their programs didn't work, and they were not easily accessible because those who designed them were culturally incompetent and oblivious to our reality of being traumatized, ostracized, and minimized.

Our kids aren't seen as kids. They need to be loved and protected by us and others who don't look like us. Unfortunately, when they see our kids, they treat them as threats, convicts, criminals, and thugs. Our kids are not given the opportunity to be innocent, but *they are*. Even in death, we are criminalized and dehumanized; I wish our lives could be respectfully memorialized.

It took me six months to stand up. I said, "If you do proactive things, you won't have to keep patting yourself on the back to save a child who's already in trouble." Frederick Douglas said it best, "It is easier to build strong children than to [try] to repair broken men [and women]."

This is the **white savior complex**...Jump in when things are wrong to save the day. We don't need saviors, we need common sense, empathy, and equity in our community [and the world at large] on every level.

After the meeting, I became visible. My voice finally mattered. They finally noticed me because they thought I needed to be saved. I decided not to be Chanae with a bachelor's degree [with titles] such as: a former banking professional, healthcare leader, successful entrepreneur, philanthropist, and humanitarian. I allowed them to see who I was, then I reintroduced myself as someone who did not need them to save me, because they couldn't. These people had to first understand the experience of being me, looking like me, feeling like me, and living *life* like me. I stripped away my 'defining accolades' because I needed them to hear me and listen actively.

Maternally, I knew it was about my children, their children and parents who looked like me. The first fallacious myth I debunked was that those who are impoverished do not any care less about their loved ones. As a matter of fact, I am convinced that they care more because their families are all they have!

Data *shouldn't* be used to weaponize, demonize or minimize a person's experience or value. Social activism isn't a checkbox or a to-do list. Each person is an individual and their circumstances are significantly different. Social change cannot be rectified without involvement from the community it impacts. Involvement must be equalized...meaning the power must be shared, and to do anything else is absolutely ludicrous!

Nothing about activism is pretty; it exceeds a catchy mantra. It's not about frilly "feel good" programs because systems [specifically, systemic racism] must be openly discussed, revisited, and reconstructed with *everyone* in mind. Activism requires applying pressure coupled with actions. Unfortunately, the same people chanting "No justice, no peace" are the same people who serve in decision-making roles at academic institutions, governments, corporations, nonprofits, faith-based organizations [and the like] who make decisions that hinder equalized justice. Who does this? People who don't give a D.A.M.N.

Chapter 1

Tokenized from the Start

I wanted to be a white girl named Stacey…

I was **tokenized**. Ironically, tokens appear to have value, but they don't have currency. Therefore, a token can only be used for the purpose "they" intended it for. There is no **agency** [just lip service] behind the actions. Lip service is not service because there's no change; subsequently, there's no impact either.

As a child, I was always quiet, and I knew something was different about my existence. My presence always caused others to be uncomfortable, and I internalized their discomfort as my own. My aim was never to be in the forefront but to always remain in the background. This kept me safe. However, I questioned who or what was I being saved from… society, family, or myself [relationally].

My parents were high school sweethearts [but very toxic by nature]. My dad was the provider for everyone. They broke up when I was four. My dad was in the Air Force and my mom was in the Navy; he was the breadwinner. He braided my hair, gave me lots of hugs and kisses. My stepmom envied his affection towards me.

He met my stepmom at the store. My mom was mad with my dad because things went south between them. My stepmom also had kids, and things were turbulent. Eventually, my mom started using drugs as a coping mechanism. She was one of the first to smoke crack cocaine. I learned to be a provider and a nurturer early on; I really didn't have much of a choice. I remember being around four-years-old and cooking corn on the stove to prepare a meal for my brother and me. My brother was precocious, and they didn't fight for him to be in gifted classes. School was our escape.

I was 12-years-old when we moved in with my aunt. There were a lot of kids in the house, and I was the oldest, I did all of the girls' hair and ran the whole household. I was the *woman* of the house. My dad called me the matriarch and I resented it because I was the middle child. The middle child typically can hide, but I couldn't; I was called to the frontlines from the beginning. As the token, I saw more and what I saw and experienced, I did not like. This is why even as an activist, I'm tokenized and conditioned for it to break barriers.

At home, my stepmom was jealous of my relationship with my dad. I was an outcast; nevertheless, ahead of my time. My Black reading teacher was hard on me and I didn't understand why she gave me so much grief [seemingly], but now I do.

So, I questioned who I was as if something was "wrong" with me. I was placed in the gifted program when I was in second-grade. I was the only Black child enrolled. I was placed among the white children and things became muddy. They accepted me but they didn't see me. While my classmates went on elaborate summer vacations, I spent my summers on Fifth Ave., reading. They were exposed to the world while I read about it and pictured it through my imagination. I played kickball at the Wilhelmina Johnson Center and the Rosa B. Community Center. Both of these centers are named after community advocates.

The naming of these centers are examples of tokenization because there was no education regarding these community icons. They were memorialized but the impact of their work was minimized. There was no sense of pride attached to the facilities. There wasn't long-term sustainable funding allocated for transformative programs. There wasn't funding to build capacity, maintenance, or upgrades. Nevertheless, we made do because that's what we've been conditioned to do [is make do].

However, my dad was never one to just *make do*. He was a supervisor at Regional Transit System and was locked up for selling drugs. I remember getting on the bus with my mom and riding to the old library. Gainesville appeared to be bustling with activity.

Dad wasn't flashy or selling drugs just to be doing it. He was providing for the family and anyone else in need. Eventually, he was sent to prison for nine years. I was nine when he was sent off and 18 when he got out.

Nevertheless, I wanted to be a white girl named Stacey, although I was just like my dad. He considered himself to be an "honest crook". My dad treated people right but according to society, he went about it the wrong way. He wasn't flashy and was one of many children who received the hand-me-downs but gave others the best. His humility exceeded his pride. He taught me how to cook chitterlings, walk me through fixing mechanical problems and he made sure everyone's needs were met.

I didn't recognize my dad's greatness then… so I thought that I wanted to be the "white girl" named Stacey because she wasn't a token. There wasn't any confusion regarding her name, and she represented the majority. Stacey was valuable and she wasn't broken [seemingly]. I wanted to be her in every sense.

Chapter 2

D.A.M.N. Disparities

D is for **disparities** and the cost we all pay [as a society] when we ignore the dangers of not addressing them. We find these in education, wages, criminal justice, housing, healthcare, access to transportation and even generational wealth [to name a few]. This is the state of despair we live in. Unfortunately, the people attempting to save us have no idea "how to do it" because they've excluded us from the process of rectification. How can "they" save us if they don't understand how to help us?

The savior complex makes whites believe they have all the power and all of the ideas and solutions. Just as children need to be saved and protected, whites believe this about Black people. Consequently, as a parent, it is my job to protect and save my children. However, what I've seen repeatedly is whites who make decisions for us then blame us when things don't work out. These decisions are made for us and without us.

In the same way Jesus is viewed as a savior; praying about it does not excuse action. Social justice exalts God; therefore, we must be doers. Christ walked with the people, worked alongside them, and trained them on the journey. The problem with programs is they do not create sustainable change and disparities aren't addressed. Therefore, around the holidays, we see Thanksgiving baskets and toy drives because these create "warm and fuzzy" feelings never getting to the root. However, again, there's no long-term change because addressing disparities is hard work and there's no room or time for self [ego] and meeting societal formalities. It is going to the root of the problem, applying pressure, holding everyone accountable and measuring outcomes, continually.

Humbly showing up with our hat in our hand asking for what's already ours isn't doing us any favors; furthermore, these distorted acts of humility won't decrease disparities; they actually increase them. Change requires us to be strategic while applying pressure from multiple levels.

When it comes to addressing disparities, make no assumptions, ask purposeful questions, and act as if you know nothing about the situation. However, preparation is still necessary. Therefore, research on the issues at hand is mandatory. A well-informed citizen is the system's worst and best enemy! This type of advocacy promotes change and at the same time reveals the looming disparities white people ignore.

I've completed research and I still research daily, so in an effort to be more informed, I allow the misinformed, egotistical representatives of the system to present *first*. This puts me on the offense so that I can strategize effectively. It helps to know what they know and what their intentions are; this helps us to learn. No matter what we're asking, we must remain humble enough to be well informed.

Even when we have all of our information, there will be times when we miss the mark. Then we must apologize quickly. This is where many get caught up, and it becomes hard for them to apologize. That's the power trip, which causes leaders to become offended by any line of questioning, especially when it's about *their* outcomes and not *ours*.

The most important question we should ask when something seems off, is *why*, followed up with lots of direct questions that are prepare in advance. Nevertheless, the process of addressing disparities is long, frustrating, and necessary. It may not be necessary to dismantle whole systems [every time] but we have to be courageously humble and diligent enough to achieve the results for our expected outcome.

My Black Son: A Disparity and a Threat?

On Wednesday, June 13, 2018, my oldest son was stopped by an Alachua County Police Officer. Prior to this event, I had the talk with my son [how to stay under the radar and how to stay alive if you're unlawfully thrown onto the radar]. My son is a high school graduate, college student, and we did everything right in hopes of preventing criminalization against him [as a Black male]. He's a great communicator and he is mild-tempered. Yet, he was still treated like a criminal.

This is why we have to change the system because even when we do things right [dot every I and cross every T], the problem isn't the person, the problem is disparities that are rooted in systemic racism, and I'm committed to changing the system.

Nevertheless, in October 2017 my son came home, and his friend came over; I smelled weed. I told him if a cop stops you and your friends, things will go south. He reassured me that it wasn't him and said, "Ma, I don't smoke."

The morning when he was pulled over, I was on the phone with him when he said, "Ma, I'm being pulled over and I don't know why." I talked him through the situation after I snapped and said, "You were probably speeding... I told you about putting the pedal to metal and you're going to pay for that damn ticket!" Then out of nowhere we heard the officer yelling from the police car's speaker. I called dispatch immediately. Then I heard my son begging and pleading with me over the phone. I lost it and knew if I didn't get there to save him, they'd kill him just like they did other innocent Black boys. It was my worst nightmare unfolding on the opposite end of the line. I told him not to hang up.

They snatched my son from the car with their guns and tasers drawn. I had a friend drive me to the scene. When we arrived, my son was handcuffed and bent over the hood of the police car. I jumped out of the car and informed the supervisor what I heard over the phone [the escalation] and he dismissed what I said. Then I asked if he was being arrested, and if so, why. I told them I worked with Gainesville for All, which is an organization that addresses racial disparities. This organization was established in response to racial disparities found in the Bebr Study facilitated by the University of Florida.

It concluded that Alachua County had the largest racial disparity in every quality-of-life indicator [there were seven categories]. Those included: access to transportation, criminal justice, education, healthcare, housing, wages, and economic development.

Surely, I believed my statement would break the ice [so I thought] but they weren't hearing me. So, I went live on FB twice. The second time, the supervisor came up and started taunting me. I told him to, "Get the fuck away from my car because we aren't friends and I'm not friendly." At that time, they were looking for a reason to arrest my 18- year-old-son but couldn't find one so they let him go. I got in my car and we drove straight to the Alachua County Sheriff's Office to file a complaint. I could tell he was traumatized... We both were.

Later that day, the sheriff had someone on her team post a video of the traffic stop with my son.

However, the video didn't have sound and this malicious act was committed by the person in power. She took an oath to serve and protect, but her actions were abusive and traumatizing. Her intention was to paint my son as a criminal. It was done in an effort to bully me, but she gave me the platform that I needed, so I used it.

I met with the sheriff a few days later and I arrived with real questions, in fact I had two days to think about it. I asked, "What do you do if you're pulled over and you are afraid?" She responded, "Call communications." I told her, "That's what we did." She responded, "It wasn't dark." I asserted, "You can't dictate the time of day when someone is afraid." Then she ignorantly responded, "His hands were aggressively holding the steering wheel." I asked, "How do you hold a steering wheel aggressively? Furthermore, it is a good thing my son followed me and not your people because our children end up dead even when they do comply!"

Finally, she admitted… "There is an issue but not within *her* organization." I countered, "When there are racial disparities, there are one of two things that must be true: either there is bias in the system or there's something wrong with *all* Black people [and the latter definitely is not true]." This statement ended our conversation, and I was unafraid because this wasn't about just my son, but it was about ALL Black boys.

This is how I became the Accidental Activist™. The charges of speeding were dropped. It was summer and the school zone speed limit was not in effect. Even if he was speeding, the situation didn't need to be escalated in that manner. I was contacted by residents of different races who said they didn't suffer this type of mistreatment.

To further prove my position, an article published in the St. Pete Times titled *Bias on the Bench,* pointed out racial disparities within the criminal justice system in Florida. The same former Alachua County Sheriff was quoted saying Blacks are more likely to be arrested because they smoke weed in public. That's a D.A.M.N. lie!

The article exposed that Blacks receive harsher/longer sentences for the same crime committed by whites. Additionally, the 2016 article states that Florida's state courts lack diversity, which is paramount when it comes to handing down sentences. Blacks make up 16 percent of Florida's population and one-third of the state's prison inmates. But fewer than seven percent of sitting judges are Black and less than half of them preside over serious felonies. White judges in Florida sentence Black defendants to 20 percent more time on average for third-degree felonies. Blacks who wear the robe give more balanced punishments.

Chapter 3

D.A.M.N. Allegiances

A is for allegiances and how ASSinine they are because the behaviors associated with them, whether they are intentional, the acts are undeniably malicious. Allegiances oppressively uphold systems that brutalize every aspect of Black existence. This starts before law enforcement interaction and it includes equalized protection of Black mothers in childbirth, healthcare disparities, educational inequities, unequal wages, lack of access to affordable housing, food disparities, school-to-prison pipeline [prison industrial complex], and police brutality.

Allegiances are often camouflaged as friendships and policies with a caveat that is supposedly beneficial to the oppressed. This is called **interest conversion**, which is also cash conversion and power conversion that leads to the shift of power. These allegiances habitually perpetuate systemic oppression.

Allegiance should not be about race, but equity. This means you have to put more effort and resources into initiatives that will close the gaps instead of widening them. Black people must stop paying allegiances to people who look like us without accountability. Black leaders often hold fast to "perceived" power, resulting in being a seat holder. These are the same elected officials who are paid to hold office, make decisions but are already powerful. Nevertheless, if we don't use power appropriately, then we're rendered powerless. Examine the track record of all leaders [Black, White, or other]. These individuals must do their job and be held accountable for outcomes that benefit *all* people, especially those who are the most vulnerable to the inequities of the systems.

Additionally, when allegiances are formed, they are formed by people who are believed to possess some perceived power. The problem with that is there is not a relinquishing of power. Power is either given up, shared, or taken. When it is taken, disparities are minimized.

Those with power have often attained it through generational wealth and war. Therefore, when people are in survival mode, they can't see past their impoverished condition. They are trying to figure out where their next meal will come from, or how to keep a roof over their heads, and simply just paying bills of necessity [just to survive]. We can't beat these individuals up for not *showing up*, because they are trying to solve *their* problems and strategizing to solve larger problems is inconceivable. However, this is why we must encourage them to vote and equip them to become their own advocates.

Nevertheless, allegiances can't be self-serving, but they must genuinely serve people. When the vulnerable gain power it's evident through economic impact. For example, my great aunt who is 76-years-old, stated, "East Gainesville had a strong community and an equally strong economy less than three decades ago because money cycled throughout our community. Unfortunately, when integration happened, *they* brutally and deceitfully took what benefited them and *they* have continually crippled our community." Again, this is interest conversion, which leads to generational distrust and worsened disparities.

As the years have passed, we've experienced **regentrification**, which is the restoration and upgrading of deteriorated urban property by middle-class or affluent people, often resulting in displacement of lower-income residents.

When generational oppression is the norm, Blacks check out because there is the belief that things will *never* change. Thereby, producing feelings of hopelessness coupled with complacency. Consequently, *we* develop a justified mentality of apathy. Being apathetic, exacerbates *the struggle* instead of eliminating the struggle. Unfortunately, this causes us to develop an individualist concern versus communal concern. Allegiances will never be mutually beneficial to all people when those who establish them are only concerned with themselves. Whether these allegiances are established among the poor, the rich, the powerful, or the powerless, the intentions may not be malicious, but they are [with the same outcome]. For instance, when an accidental killing occurs, someone is *still* dead; although the intent wasn't death, the outcome is *still* malicious, and families suffer.

Nevertheless, our interests must come first. We must present what we want, our way. We must take a seat at the table. So, while the powerful may offer assistance, we must hold the vision and execute the plan. This is a new way of thinking. Sadly, when we are accustomed to being grateful for scraps; because of our disparities, we accept a little bit as a lot and further believe that something is better than nothing.

For instance, that funky ass $600 stimulus check "given" by the government as "help" is a prime example of *scraps*. It took governmental leaders nine months to negotiate whether to give these scraps to the American people. Now this is a D.A.M.N. shame!

So, fuck these self-serving, hypocritical, egotistical, supercilious, and obsequious individuals who only do what they do in an effort to be even *more* powerful. Thereby, our allegiances must be to reformative changes to rectify and improve our society. Our allegiances cannot be given to systems, institutions, and ideals of oppression that keep us subjugated.

Ironically, I stopped saying the pledge of allegiance and stopped singing the national anthem when I was in fourth grade. I realized after conducting research that these public displays of allegiance should have only been recited by *them*, because it only applied to *them* White Anglo Saxon Protestants [WASP]. Research Francis Bellamy.

I believe now is the time for us to seriously consider who and what we pledge our allegiance to and why. Especially after the insurrection that took place in the U.S. Capitol Building Wednesday, January 6, 2021 by White thugs, and terrorists [not patriots]. Patriots are individuals who have national pride, with an embedded sense of respect. These individuals are attachment to "their" homeland and possess an alliance with citizens who share the same sentiment. This attachment is a combination of many different feelings relative to a homeland, including ethnic, cultural, political, or historical aspects. However, patriotism only benefits the majority.

The insurrection is also an example of how dangerous allegiances are. When allegiances benefit the powerful, these individuals become threatened because they are the benefactors of the privilege it creates. Additionally, allegiances to institutions, religion/religious organizations are equally detrimental.

However, when allegiances are not self-serving, but purposely serve the powerless, then and only then can allegiances be beneficial to everyone. It is imperative that those in power recognize that their "power" cannot remain disproportionately imbalanced; because the benefit of the power keeps *them* powerful and renders us even more powerless. This further paralyzes us at all levels because there is no partnership but a dictatorship.

At one point in time, people had mutually beneficial allegiances to churches and vice versa. When churches lack partnership, the religious politics exclude justice. This is abominable. Undeniably, God wants us to be happy, free, stable, fruitful, and blessed. Without justice we will not experience any of these things and ultimately continue a cycle of suffering.

This commentary will probably piss some people off. However, being pissed-off is actually a good thing because when people are mad or uncomfortable, in response to an issue/concern, there's a reassessment of thoughts and actions that happen.

Case in point, I actually grappled with my love of God, church, and religion. Actually, I hate religion because it is *about* God but *without* God. Religion is used to oppress and start wars and breed hate. I refuse to be a part of it!

For years, I thought that something was wrong with me because I loved God, yet I was so turned off;

although, I always acknowledged God. I am however, vehemently opposed to the negative connotation associated with religion and church. It is more and more evident that people are religiously lost and that's a D.A.M.N. shame! Sadly, those of us who say we have found Christ are supposed to be salt, light, and sugar in the world. So, what does this really mean?

When we are salt (not salty) we understand how vital we are to others. Salt is an essential nutrient that is necessary to preserve life. It also is used to disinfect things that are dirty. So, if we are to be salt, our actions will show that Christ is necessary in our lives. We will work to preserve God's word and clean up the things that the world has tarnished—starting with ourselves. How can we be salt (or anything positive) if we are always looking down and condemning others? We need to renew our D.A.M.N. mindset!

Additionally, we are charged with guiding people that are in darkness to the light. There should be mounting evidence that God is present in our lives. The evidence should be stacked against us and we should all be found guilty as charged for being like Christ. Joy should emit from our spirits without us having to utter a word about God.

How can we bring light to darkness if we refuse to acknowledge it? It is necessary to understand why people are in darkness *if* God's light is supposed to penetrate it. If we always judge and ridicule people, how can our light illuminate anything?

If we're going to be sugar to the world, we must be sweet; being sweet and humble is not the same as being a doormat. We must ask God for wisdom on how to be sweet when others may or may not receive us or our message. This is one of the greatest vices in my own life. How can we be sweet (not fake) to someone that we feel does not deserve it? Following Gods' word will reveal the answers. Does any of this mean perfection? HELL NO, because we are all imperfect people who fall short!

Fortunately, in God's eyes, we are all equal. We are human, we make mistakes and God still loves us, *unconditionally.* Therefore, we should do the same for others.

Who I am now is better than who I was, and who I am becoming is better than who I am now. However, I am better than no one. Neither religion nor church changed me— God did! If God hadn't worked on my heart and mind, I would never have made it to a church. God works to change people through us. We must *work* to be vessels who carry God's love and amazing grace.

It is impossible to serve and please God if we are tearing down God's people (and we're all HIS people). Undoubtedly, *every* saint has a past, and every sinner has a future.

Therefore, we must understand that the allegiances we are loyal to, (religiously, politically, educationally, socially, personally, or professionally) are the very things that will catapult us or cripple us, it is our choice. So, if we are going to pledge allegiance to anything… our loyalty must be to things that prove we truly give a D.A.M.N.

This is our **D.A.M.N.** Pledge of Allegiance [say it loud and proud].

I will not pledge my allegiance to systems, institutions, and ideals that promote and willingly implement practices of oppression in good conscience. Therefore, I will intentionally educate myself regarding the disparities, allegiances, and mindsets that have not and do not gainfully advance people who have endured and continue to endure oppression while simultaneously attempting to defeat it. So, I pledge allegiance to true justice, true liberation, and true equality.

This pledge of allegiance is worth reciting!

Chapter 4

D.A.M.N. Mindsets

Mindsets are shaped by cultural values, norms, and traditions. Some of us keep the same mindset because we believe changing our minds indicates disloyalty. It is amazing how our mindsets and even unspoken rules cause us to remain loyal to people, habits, and ideas that do not benefit us or help rectify the issues we face. We do it because "It's what we've always done." And if it's what we've always done, the question is, has our unchanged mindset rendered beneficial changes in our lives, in the lives of our family, and in our communities? If the answer to this question is no, then you need to change your D.A.M.N. mind, now!

Take for instance, the unspoken rule that a "lady" *shouldn't* "cuss." Well, I do. In fact, I think we all should cuss... shhhhiiit. In fact, we should teach our girls to cuss, let's call it **code switching**. I know this isn't considered "lady-like". Some would even say, the use of profanity deems us somewhat classless because we've broken one of the rules of being a "lady". However, sometimes we have to be profane to be profound. Profanity is a universal language everyone understands.

Therefore, it's necessary to start fires, ruffle some feathers and cause a damn tsunami if we must; thereby, we proudly embrace being the **disrupters** who produce change. So, if I say, "you gave me a hard time", that's one thing, but if I say, "you fucked me over", you fully understand what I meant. You will experience my pain and possibly understand my frustration!

Nevertheless, girls need to know that if being "lady-like" or nice doesn't serve them and following the policies/rules doesn't yield their expected outcome; then girls and women need to know how to tell those who are challenging them [for all the wrong reasons] where to get off.

In a world that has shaped the rules and roles for women and minorities to stay in their place, profanity not only gets a person's undivided attention, but they will finally listen, especially when we have receipts. Yes, as a Black woman, we will be labeled as angry or even ghetto, but we're far from stupid even if we do cuss.

Despite the stereotypes, according to the National Center for Education Statistics, the most educated group in America is Black women. Additionally, Black women have earned more advanced degrees than any other group. So, when we cuss, it's not an indication of ignorance, but a display of our frustration. Tell me who is nice when they are angry, abused, brutalized, traumatized, and dismissed? Whites are often entitled to their rage and their anger is justified and then ridiculously minimized. We hear it all the time, "He didn't mean it, he just blew a fuse" or "She lost it a little," or "He just killed nine people at a Black church and was taken for a meal because he said he was hungry." However, for us, everyone runs scared when we say, "that's bullshit", "kiss my ass" or "fuck all of that."

Our frustrations are valid because we are tired of seeing Black men unjustly killed on the evening news or because we're raising Black sons [whom we're trying to protect], or we didn't get the promotion that we rightfully deserved. Or we landed the job and the salary we received is 30 percent less than our white counterparts; although we're more qualified. Carrying this kind of weight frustrates the shit out of us! Therefore, our respect for them is dismissed because they've already disrespected us. Again, being amicable is a form of compliance and submission, particularly for Black women regardless of what's happening.

Another mindset that we must address is the idea of apologizing without changed behavior. Black people stop apologizing and being afraid of our blackness and our greatness. Apologies do not rectify the issues within systems that are ladened with institutionalized racism. Why apologize without leveling the playing field? White people you should apologize for not using your privilege to ensure purposeful change.

We must change the mindset of believing that if we just remain quiet things will play out the way they should. That's D.A.M.N. stupid! Even when it comes to voting, some people want us to feel run down and hopeless, so we won't vote. However, as a people who had everything taken from us, elections give us the same power as everyone else. Therefore, we must advocate for ourselves in an effort to protect ourselves from further abuse through misrepresentation or anything else that continues to deem us unworthy and powerless.

Oh, and white media, you need to be ashamed, too, because you uphold detrimental stereotypes yet reveal the truth about America's ugly history. You're the culprit that keeps things the same. The media humanizes white murderers and rapists, but Blacks aren't even humanized in death. Only in America are Blacks killed, criminalized, and convicted because of our blackness. Sadly, this is the norm. We are blamed for our unjustified deaths, the media diminishes our humanity, and we are never presumed innocent but ALWAYS guilty! This is also a D.A.M.N. shame!

Law enforcement officers and news reporters portray white shooters as victims and martyrs. Why? Is the hope of gaining sympathy initiated because they are white? News flash: contrary to popular belief, white DOES NOT mean right. So, put down the violins, and let's reveal the true narrative. The justification of whiteness and **white violence** perpetuates Black deaths; thereby, criminalizing and dehumanizing Black victims to justify the crimes of white thugs within the systems. Now that's some S.H.I.T. - sideways, hypocritical, ignorant, thinking!

The justification of white violence goes right back to the way they took land from indigenous people (Native Americans) and the way they justified slavery [the slaughter and rape of our people]. Again, the insurrection on January 6, 2021, was more white violence. It is a system, like racism and capitalism. Therefore, when violent acts are committed against Blacks, it is justified by white people in power. This is why we must change our D.A.M.N. mindsets to create a power shift.

A D.A.M.N. Changed Mindset Checklist

- **Be in relationships and not relation*shit*** - If you curse someone out every day, that's some toxic shit. Let them have it, let them win, and keep your peace. Simply acknowledge the fact that you are not for everyone.

- **Be wealthy and healthy** (quantity vs. quality) - If you haven't put some money aside for a rainy day, start today because it could be raining later on. Wealth is more than money. It is quality of life. We should be investing in our spiritual and mental health. Take walks, drink water, eat healthy. Deal with your trauma. It is OK to seek counseling; it's one of the best investments you'll make. Show up for yourself because no one else can advocate for you.

Although, money doesn't cure all things. Think about how many celebrities have drug addictions and succumb to them. If money were the "cure-all" they wouldn't have the addictions or some of them would still be here. Even professional athletes who "make it out" and become rich, they don't manage their money well because no one enriches them. So, they have money without sustainable wealth. Wealth requires a tribal mindset. We're only as wealthy as the impact we make. Impact is our greatest wealth.

- **Be investors and save** - Time out for everybody scraping up money to bury somebody's Black ass. No more GoFundMe funerals (they take eight percent of the money raised anyways). Just cut out the middleman. It only cost $50 a month for a funky little life insurance policy. Save some money and invest in enough insurance to ensure the loved ones (particularly minors) are taken care of.

- **Be loud** - Make noise about shit you know ain't right and mobilize others to help raise hell until the wrong is made right.

- **Be Passionate** - Get off the damn sidelines and become passionate about something in your community. We can no longer justify doing nothing when the cause is valid. We still need to help when we can and don't complain about your efforts.

- **Be more than religious** - Saints get all caught up on how things look; therefore, they choose not to get involved. This is the wrong D.A.M.N. mindset. David was a bastard, but God loved him because of his heart. When it was time for him to fight Goliath, people thought he was crazy. So, when the battle doesn't look like it's worth fighting, sometimes we don't show up. Who decides which battles are worth fighting and when we should show up? Checks and balances for showing up starts with changing our mindset. Black religious folk, you're the problem. When the question is posed, what would Jesus do? My response is, get up off His ass and do something, which He did!

For example, trash was left at a public building Easter weekend and it made the local Gainesville news. White people leave trash all the time during Bike Week and Art Festivals, but we'll say, "That's why they won't give us anything." The reality is, there's no place for us to go where we feel welcome. And the places we can go, they won't accept us. However, we must see ourselves as worthy of having our own and being in those places. We are better than appearing at the top of the newscast wailing because of another senseless murder of someone who looks like us.

- **Be strong and vulnerable** - Strength and vulnerability are one in the same. We are programmed to worry about what people think or minimize who we are. Being vulnerable allows you to connect with those who need you the most. We must find our weak spots and partner with those who are strong in our areas of weakness.

- **Be effective communicators** - For so long being silent was the means of survival (it was either life or death). Therefore, we had to be quiet to show compliance and prove our worthiness. We kept our mouths shut to keep our "piece of job", stay in schools, live in substandard housing, and appear invisible.

Additionally, silence has been woven into our culture and as a result we have superficial conversations. When we communicate, we must get to the bottom of our issues. Whatever we do, let's communicate about having a will and what will happen to grandma's house when she passes away. Keeping the home creates wealth for us, and don't forget to pay the property taxes.

Chanae Jackson

Chapter 5

D.A.M.N. N-Words

I don't think we should retire using the N-word. Besides, who told us we should stop using it? Again, this is interest conversion. Should we use it only in the presence of our own people or when we feel like it? When people hear the word nigga, what they hear is nigger. Regardless of what they hear, they only think of the word's history and not its evolution.

No, Nancy, you don't get to use this word because it ain't your damn word! Truthfully, I could care less if you use the word because name calling is a distraction. It's your actions that precede and follow the use of this word that matters. Calling me the N-word and treating me like one are two different things.

Black folks, we can't get wrapped up in the chatter. We get our revenge when we hold our dollars, invest in our communities and vote. However, if you treat me like

41

a nigga by intentionally preventing me from getting a promotion, we have a problem. Glass ceilings are meant to be shattered, even if we're cut by the shards on impact.

Take President Obama, he was the first Black to hold the office of president, yet he was deemed the worse by many. He and his wife were heavily scrutinized by the media. President Obama was ridiculed for wearing a tan suit, Michele was scorned for wearing sleeveless dresses/tops and for touching the Queen of England. It was all a distraction.

This takes me to my next N-word, *needs*. We all have them, however, when the basic needs of anyone aren't met, it points back to broken systems. Unapologetically, these systems show that our humanity means *nothing*, and they treat us as though we are *nothing*. This is further exemplified by the actions of the "powers that be" to create/sustain counterproductive systems and beliefs. This is **white violence**, the legal, intentional, and brutal raping of us educationally, socially, financially, and politically.

The systems are intentionally designed this way to maintain control instead of promoting and ensuring communities are healthy. For example, the intent of the judicial system isn't to create "safer" communities that are so-called "healthy" communities. However, healthy communities are *always* safe because needs are met.

Institutionalized racism is not justice. **Incrementalism** is not justice. **Solidarity** is not justice. **White Savior Complex** is not justice. **Misplaced vengeance** is not justice. Allow me to educate you about what justice really is and what it looks like. Justice fosters hope and provides the balance of power that is needed for necessary and purposeful change. Justice should be the core of every community. When it is non-existent our communities are ladened with police brutality, the harshest sentencing, corrupt and self-pleasing politicians, dilapidated and/or unaffordable housing, biased educational practices, and rehabilitation programs that don't rehabilitate anything or anyone... they simply perpetuate faulty and unproductive cycles.

Additionally, when our needs are unmet, unhealthy outcomes are unavoidable. Our untreated anxiety and undiagnosed PTSD manifests negatively and causes our people to suffer from obesity, substance abuse, **violent survival**, **brainwashed hoteps**, and unproductive compliance that leads to complacency.

So, before we proceed to the next *N-word*, I need my readers to close your mouths, open your ears, and expand your **capacity** to not only think, but to think beyond the boxes that have been created by society and yourselves. Don't get stuck on that one "n-word" and totally dismiss and ignore the other "*N-words*" that irrefutably affect our well-being like: *naivety*, saying no (and meaning it); minimizing neglect (of yourself and others); and understanding the *non-negotiables* while abstaining from condescending *nastiness*.

Time's up for using *naivety* as an excuse for not showing up and showing OUT. Change doesn't just happen...then again, it happens all the time— often at our expense, it is never the changes that we want or need... ONLY what *they* want.

Naivety includes three groups of people. The first group is the innocently ignorant. I get it, some people really do not know what's going on. They've completely checked out. The second group includes people who know what's going on but don't want to compromise their quality of life. Then there are the MFs who feel as if they've "arrived," and they don't want to sabotage their *perceived* privilege. Again, our wealth is only as resourceful as the communities we serve.

We've all heard that it cost us nothing to be *nice* — and it doesn't. Speak, smile, and encourage somebody. Niceness and kindness are first cousins if not siblings. These are expressions (followed by actions). In my opinion, being nice equates to showing up to move chairs, helping with spreadsheets, babysitting for a meeting, making food, donating to pay rent for a soon to be evicted neighbor. The great news is... all of these things are already happening; all you have to do is show up, smile, listen, and jump right in. Life can and will challenge us all, but being nice will require effort some days, but do not throw in the towel. Black folks, we have always had to fight. So, let's stop fighting each other and if we must exchange words (even if we cuss a little), let's leave it alone, accept different opinions, and be diplomatic about it.

#DiplomaticDisrespect

My final N-word is NO, please understand it is a complete sentence. We must say NO to the following:

- No to accepting scraps

- No to begging/pleading for a seat at certain tables

- No to alliances and allegiances

- No to apathy

- No to anything that minimizes or shuts down your voice

- No to complaining without solutions

- No to distractions and dysfunction

- No to giving information for free and there's no return in our communities

- No to microaggressions and discriminatory workplace practices

- No to asking: Know what you want and demand it

- No to nastiness

- No to reckless spending and yes to saving and investing

- No to respectability

- No to staying home during elections (run your ass to the polls)!

- No to systems and the way things are

- No to toxic relationships

Simply put, just say no to anything that doesn't challenge us, change us, change our communities, and nation for the better.

Chapter 6

Be a D.A.M.N. Good Activist

According to Merriam Webster Dictionary an activist is defined as a one who advocates or practices **activism**; a person who uses or supports strong actions (such as public protests) in support of or opposition to one side of a controversial issue. Additionally, all citizens born into any society should contribute to the necessary changes that are needed to ensure political, social, educational, and economical balance of power.

However, to be a D.A.M.N. good activist, first you must give a D.A.M.N. You cannot idly sit on the sidelines talking about what could be done or what should be done or better yet who is doing it and how they're doing it wrong! Get off yo ass and do it! If you're not part of the solution, you are an irrefutable part of the problem!

It doesn't matter if you're an average, everyday person at some point in your life, you will become a

D.A.M.N. activist, and I hope you'll become a good one! Activism is not intimidating as it may seem; however, all it requires is action. The actions can be simplistic as making a phone call, checking on an elderly neighbor, or speaking up about something you know is dead wrong!

Yes, you will have to stand up for something. In fact, I believe that all of us are called [in some capacity] to assume our position as a D.A.M.N. activist! As fighters for those who are powerless, activists hold the powerful fully accountable. We make noise and waves and cause change. Although, you may not be as loud as I am, the noise you make will be heard and ultimately felt!

So, research policies, review emails, make calls, read news articles, and assess the validity of various sources. Remember the names of key stakeholders you've spoken with and know who the right stakeholders are and how to connect with them.

It is our responsibility to know what policies, procedures, and initiatives these stakeholders are responsible for and how they can either help or hinder progress within our communities. We must also hold these individuals accountable to their own D.A.M.N. policies. When we are well-informed regarding the issues that affect us, it eliminates the possibility of being hoodwinked and bamboozled by the powers that be. Thus, placing us in a position to be forceful agents of change.

As influential change-agents, developing and establishing mutually beneficial relationships are vital! In other words, the power must be balanced and not one-sided, which causes a continual see-saw effect. The powerful remain high and inaccessible to those they're supposed to help and the powerless remain low while they try to access those in power.

If change is going to happen and be sustained in our society the scales of justice and power must be balanced. Too many of us are sick and tired of being sick and tired. We are tired of waiting for a change to come, and Sam Cooke sounds too damn sad anyway! It is time to turn this MF out! So, join me in being a D.A.M.N. good activist— intentionally!

Glossary

1. **Activism** - the policies and actions of using vigorous and strategic campaigning to bring about political or social change.

2. **Agency** – the capacity of individuals to act independently and to make their own free choices. By contrast, structure are those factors of influence (such as social class, religion, gender, ethnicity, ability, customs, etc.) that determine or limit agents and their decisions.

3. **Brainwashed Hoteps** - a person who's either a clueless parody of Afrocentricity" or "loudly, conspicuously and obnoxiously pro-black but anti-progress." These are Black people who believe that sexist responsibility, politics, and gender roles are pillars of honor and tools to overthrow racism.

4. **Capacity** - the ability of individuals in a democracy to become active citizens and to work together to solve collective problems and of communities to encourage such participation in their members.

5. **Code Switching** - process of shifting from one linguistic **code** (a language or dialect) to another, depending on the **social** context or conversational setting.

6. **Disparity** - the rights or opportunities that must be available to everyone, but for obviously inequitable reasons they are not such as: race, socioeconomic status, political association, education, and housing.

7. **Disrupters** – people who are intentional and outcome-driven that go against the grain or what's been "accepted" socially and they know it is the right thing to do because change is necessary.

8. **Incrementalism** - the rejection of a rational, comprehensive model of decision-making that requires careful articulation of all goals and full consideration of all alternatives for the benefit of the effected group.

9. **Interest Conversion** – the malicious facade of friendships and policies with a caveat that is supposedly beneficial to the oppressed. However, the power conversion within it leads to the shift of power that usually makes the powerful even more powerful and renders the powerless with less power.

10. **Institutionalized Racism**- a form of **racism** that is embedded through laws within society or an organization. It can lead to such issues as **discrimination** **in** criminal justice,

employment, housing, health care, political power, and education, among other issues.

11. **Misplaced Vengeance** - the unjustifiable punishment or retaliation that is inflicted upon those who have been victimized and ostracized by those in power and those with perceived power.

12. **Regentrification** - the act or process of regentrifying while **gentrification** is the process of renewal and rebuilding accompanying the influx of middle class or affluent people into deteriorating areas that often displaces the poorer residents of that community.

13. **Solidarity** - is an awareness of shared interests, objectives, standards, and sympathies creating a psychological sense of unity of groups or classes. It refers to the ties in a society that bind people together as one.

14. **Tokenized**- the practice of making only a perfunctory or symbolic effort to be inclusive to members of minority groups, especially by recruiting people from underrepresented groups in order to give the appearance of racial or gender equality within a workplace or educational context.

15. **White Savior Complex** - is the idea that people who benefit from white privilege help those in

underserved communities for their own benefit more than that of the communities. White Savior Complex is not about justice. It is about having a big emotional experience that validates/justifies white privilege.

16. **White Violence** - the legal, intentional, and brutal raping of Black people educationally, socially, financially, and politically.

17. **Violent Survival** – the desperate and often scarce survival of Black people because of disparities; This survival sometimes include illegal activities that often leads to unavoidable legal ramifications.

About the Author

Chanae Jackson, is not just the Accidental Activist™, she is also a mother, a daughter, a sister, a friend, a community leader [who is definitely for the streets], a philanthropist, a serial entrepreneur, and now the world-renowned author of, "Yeah, I Said It, I Don't Give a D.A.M.N. Addressing: Disparities, Allegiances, Mindsets, and the N-words."

Chanae's audaciousness and willingness has NOT allowed her to just talk about change. However, she epitomizes what change is and she shows others what is required to be a change agent. Ms. Jackson isn't sorry regarding the manner in which she leads, teaches, and ensures beneficial outcomes. Chanae is the embodiment of what it means to be a true activist, intentionally.

She is a graduate of Saint Leo University and holds a Bachelor's degree in psychology. Chanae is also a licensed real estate agent. In her spare time, she's spending quality time with her family, traveling, and curling up with a good book at home or possibly at the beach.